ITALIAN SLANGUAGE

A FUN VISUAL GUIDE TO ITALIAN TERMS AND PHRASES BY MIKE ELLIS

DEDICATED TO ALL THOSE WHO THOUGHT LEARNING ITALIAN WAS DIFFICULT.

First Edition
16 15 14 13   5 4

Text © 2012 Mike Ellis
Illustrations © 2012 Rupert Bottenberg, except
illustration of trumpet player on page 59, and
illustration of heart on pages 46 and 67

Published by
Gibbs Smith
P.O. Box 667
Layton, Utah 84041

1.800.835.4993 orders
www.gibbs-smith.com

Designed by michelvrana.com
Gibbs Smith books are printed on paper produced
from sustainable PEFC-certified forest/controlled
wood source. Learn more at www.pefc.org.
Printed and bound in Hong Kong

Library of Congress Cataloging-in-Publication
Data

Ellis, Mike, 1961-
   Italian slanguage : a fun visual guide to Italian
terms and phrases / Mike Ellis. — 1st ed.
       p. cm.
   ISBN 978-1-4236-2491-2
1. Italian language—Conversation and phrase
books—English. 2. Italian language—Spoken
Italian. I. Title.
   PC1121.E44 2012
   458.3'421—dc23
                                        2012001435

CONTENTS

HOW TO USE THIS BOOK

If you have always wanted to learn the basics of Italian, but traditional methods seemed overwhelming or intimidating, this book is for you! Just follow the directions below and soon you'll be able to say dozens of words and phrases in Italian.

• Follow the illustrated prompts and say the phrase quickly and smoothly. Emphasize the words or syllables highlighted in red.

• Learn to string together words or phrases to create many more phrases.

• Draw your own pictures to help with memorization and pronunciation.

Note: This book may produce Americanized Italian.

For free sound bytes, visit slanguage.com.

GREETINGS AND RESPONSES

Hello/goodbye *Ciao*	**Chow**
Goodbye *Arrivederci*	**Odd Eva Dare Chee**
Good evening *Buonasera*	**Bonus Said a**
What is your name? *Come ti chiami?*	**Comb Met Tee Key Ah Me?**

My name is . . .
Mi chiamo . . .

Me Key Ah Moe . . .

Where do you live?
Dove vivi?

Dove Vay Vee Vee?

May I?
Posso?

Poe Sew?

How are you?
Come stai?

Comb Mess Tie?

How's it going?
Come va?

Comb May Va?

Are you well?
Stai bene?

Sty Benny?

Well
Bene

Benny

Very well
Molto bene

Mole Toe Benny

So so
Così così

Cozy Cozy

Fairly well
Abbastanza bene

Abba Stuns Up Benny

Where are you from?
Di dove sei?

Dee Dove Ace Say?

What a beautiful . . .
Che bella . . .

Kay Bell Ah . . .

I don't know
Non so

Known Sew

Welcome
Benvenuto

Ben Ven New Toe

What's his name?
Come si chiama?

Comb Mess See Key Ah Ma?

His name is . . .
Si chiama . . .

See Key Ah Ma . . .

What's new?
Che c'e di nuovo?

Kay Chay Dee New Oh Voe?

You're welcome
Prego

Pray Go

In my opinion
Secondo me

Say Cone Doe May

Help
Aiuto

Eye You Toe

Sister in law *Cognata*	 **Cone Yacht a**
Child *Bambina*	 **Bomb Been a**
Daughter *Figlia*	**Feel Ya**
Son *Figlio*	**Feel Yo**

Grandmother *Nonna*	**Known a**
Grandfather *Nonno*	**No No**
Grandparents *Nonni*	**No Knee**
Husband *Marito*	**Mod Eat Toe**

Uncle
Zio

Zee Oh

Aunt
Zia

Zee a

Grandchildren
Nipoti

Knee Poe Tee

Twin
Gemello

Gem Mellow

FOOD AND RESTAURANTS

May I have . . .
Desidero . . .

Daisy Dade Oh ...

Beer
Birra

Bee'd a

Drinks
Bibita

Bee Bee Tah

Coffee
Caffè

Café

Chocolate
Cioccolato

Choke Coal Lot Toe

Wine
Vino

Vee No

Cup
Tazza

Tot's a

Breakfast
Colazione

Coal Lot See Owe Neigh

Cheese
Formaggio

4 Ma Joe

Beef
Bistecca

Bee Steak a

Chicken
Pollo

Polo

Meat
Carne

Car Neigh

Salmon
Salmone

 Sal Moe Neigh

French fries
Patatine fritte

Pot Tot Tina Free Tay

Glass
Bicchiere

Bee Key Eddie

Knife
Coltello

Coal Tell Oh

To cook *Cucinare*	**Coo Chee Nod Eh**
Pepper *Pepe*	**Pay Pay**
Lollipop *Lecca lecca*	**Lick a Lick a**
Onion *Cipolla*	**Cheap Pole a**

Peas
Piselli

Pea Sell Lee

Potato
Patata

Pot Tot Ta

Butter
Burro

Boo'd Oh

Tomato
Pomodoro

Poe Moe Dodo

Ice Cream
Gelato

Gel Lot Toe

Apple
Mela

Mail a

Plate
Piatto

Pea Yacht Toe

Bottle
Bottiglia

Bow Teal Yah

Waiter
Cameriere

Come Eddie Eddie

Delicious
Delizioso

Dell Eat See Owe Sew

Banana
Banana

Banana

Melon
Melone

May Low Neigh

Lemon
Limone

Lee Moe Neigh

Sauce
Salsa

Salsa

Spaghetti
Spaghetti

Spaghetti

Menu
Menù

May New

Expensive *Caro*	**Cod Oh**
Money *Soldi*	**Sole Dee**
Check *Assegno*	**Us Sane Yo**
Store *Magazzino*	**Maggot See No**

Shop
Negozio

Cash
Contanti

The dress
Il vestito

Neigh Goat See Oh

Cone Ton Tee

Eel Vest Tee Toe

TRAVEL AND GEOGRAPHY

Train
Treno

Train Oh

Station
Stazione

Stott See Owe Neigh

Airport
Aeroporto

Ed Oh Pour Toe

Airplane
Aeroplano

Ed Oh Plan Oh

Ticket
Biglietto

Bee'll Yet Toe

Bus
Autobus

Owe Toe Booze

Departure
Partenza

Par 10's Ah

Jet
Jet

Jet

Underground
Metropolitana

Metro Polly Tah Nah

Taxi
Taxi

Tock See

Restaurant
Ristorante

Rest Oh Ron Tay

Where is the bathroom?
Dov'é il bagno?

Doe Vay Eel Bun Yo?

Motorcycle
Motocicletta

Moto Cheek Letta

Bicycle
Bicicletta

Bee Cheek Letta

Beautiful city
Bella città

Bell Ah Cheetah

Seat
Posto

Post Oh

| Dangerous | **Petty Coal Low Sew** |
| *Pericoloso* | |

| Zoo | **Zoo** |
| *Zoo* | |

| Hotel | **Oh Tell** |
| *Hotel* | |

| Hospital | **Oh Spay Dolly** |
| *Ospedale* | |

Gas station *Benzinaio*	**Ben Zee Now**
Castle *Castello*	**Cuss Tell Oh**
Church *Chiesa*	 **Key Yes a**
Museum *Museo*	**Moo Say Oh**

The lake
Il lago

Eel Log Oh

German
Tedesco

Ted Desk Oh

Canadian
Canadese

Con Nod Day Say

Chinese
Cinese

Chee Neigh Say

Italian
Italiano

Eat Tolly Ah No

Mexican
Messicano

Messy Con Oh

Bell Joe

Belgium
Belgio

Canada
Canada

Canada

United States
Stati Uniti

Stott Tee You Knee Tee

Italy
Italia

Eat Tail Ya

Mexico
Messico

Messy Coe

World
Mondo

Moan Doe

West
Ovest

Oh Vest

East
Est

A ♠ Ace'd

North
Nord

Nord

South
Sud

Sue'd

Accountant
Contabile

Cone Top Bee Lay

Doctor
Medico

May Dee Coe

Mechanic
Meccanico

May Connie Coe

Police officer
Poliziotto

Poe Leet See Oh Toe

Mail carrier
Postino

Post Tee No

Garbage collector
Spazzino

Spot See No

Physicist
Fisico

Fee Seek Oh

Musician
Musicista

Moosey Cheese Tah

Soldier
Soldato

Sole Dot Toe

Banker
Banchiere

Bong Key Eddie

Boss
Capo

Cop Oh

HOUSEHOLD

Dishwasher
Lavapiatti

Love Up Pea Yacht Tee

Bed
Letto

Lay Toe

Washing machine
Lavastoviglie

Lava Stove Veal Yay

Furniture
Mobile

Moe Bee Lay

Carpet
Tappeto

Top Pay Toe

Sheet
Foglio

Foal Yo

Oven
Forno

4 Know

Bedroom
Camera da letto

Come Aid a Doll Let Toe

Dishes
Piatti

Pea Yacht Tee

Comfortable
Comodo

Comb Oh Doe

Bath
Bagno

Bun Yo

Mirror
Specchio

Spay Key Oh

Curtain *Tenda*	**Tenda**
Video *Video*	**Vee Day Oh**
Balcony *Balcone*	**Ball Cone Neigh**

PRONOUNS, PREPOSITIONS, AND CONJUNCTIONS

I *Io*	**E.O.**	
You *Tu*	**2**	
He *Lui*	**Louie**	
She *Lei*	**Lay**	

We
Noi

No Way

They
Loro

Load Oh

Who?
Chi?

Key?

Everybody
Tutti

2 Tee

All
Tutto

2 Toe

Whose
Di chi

Dee Key

But
Ma

Ma

If
Se

Say

With
Con

Cone

On
Su

Sue

Under
Sotto

Sew Toe

Around
Intorno

In Tore No

Until
Fino

Fee No

Say Cone Doe

According to
Secondo

Where
Dove

Doe Vay

How?
Come?

Comb May?

After
Dopo

Dope Oh

As well as
Così come

Cozy Comb May

Just
Solo

Solo

So
Così

Cozy

ADJECTIVES AND ADVERBS

Ordinary
Comune

Comb Moo Neigh

New
Nuovo

New Oh Voe

Alone
Solo

Solo

Usual
Solito

Sew Lee Toe

Silent
Silenzioso

See Lane See Oh Sew

Same
Stesso

Stay Sew

Complete
Completo

Comb Play Toe

Of course
Certo

Chair Toe

Very
Molto

Mole Toe

Well
Bene

Benny

Only
Solo

Solo

Often
Spesso

Space Oh

By the way . . .
Comunque . . .

Comb Moon Kay ...

How?
Come?

Comb May?

Who?
Chi?

Key?

Better
Meglio

Mel Yo

Less
Meno

May No

More
Più

Pea You

Fluently
Fluentemente

Fluent Tame Men Tay

Silently
Silenziosamente

See Lane See Owes a Men Tay

Even though . . .
Nonostante . . .

No No Stun Tay ...

Next
Prossimo

Pro See Moe

After
Dopo

Dope Oh

Early
Presto

Press Toe

Late
Tardi

Tardy

At least
Almeno

All May No

Slowly
Lentamente

Len Tom Men Tay

Small
Piccolo

Pea Coal Oh

ch

Ed Oh Sew

Handsome
Bello

Bellow

Engaged
Fidanzato

Fee Done's Ah Toe

Good
Buono

Bono

Dear
Caro

Cod Oh

Nice
Gentile

Jen Tee Lay

Talkative
Chiacchierone

Key Yucky Ed Oh N

Calm
Calmo

Call Moe

Boring
Noioso

No We Oh Sew

Crazy
Pazzo

Pot Sew

Unhappy
Infelice

In Fail Ea

Thoughtful
Pensieroso

Pain See

Clumsy
Goffo

Go Foe

Dishonest
Disonesto

Dee Sew Nest Oh

Honest
Onesto

Owe Nest Oh

Well-dressed
Ben vestito

Ben Vest Tee Toe

Crazy
Pazzo

Pot Sew

Unhappy
Infelice

In Fail Each

Thoughtful
Pensieroso

Pain See Ed Oh Sew

Clumsy
Goffo

Go Foe

Hard-working
Lavoratore

Love Owed a Toe'd Eh

Stupid
Stupido

Stew Pea Doe

Outgoing
Espansivo

Ace Pun See Voe

Generous
Generoso

Jay Nade Oh Sew

Nice
Gentile

Jen Tee Lay

Talkative
Chiacchierone

Key Yucky Ed Oh Neigh

Calm
Calmo

Call Moe

Boring
Noioso

No We Oh Sew

Handsome
Bello

Bellow

Engaged
Fidanzato

Fee Done's Ah Toe

Good
Buono

Bono

Dear
Caro

Cod Oh

Blue
Blu

Blue

Black
Nero

Neigh'd Oh

Red
Rosso

Roe Sew

White
Bianco

Bee Young Coe

NUMBERS AND TIME

Thousand *Mille*	**Me Lay**
Million *Milione*	**Mealy Oh Neigh**
Billion *Miliardo*	**Me Lee Are Doe**
Half *Mezzo*	**Met Sew**

Usually
Di solito

Dee Sew Lee Toe

Tomorrow
Domani

Doe Ma Knee

Day after tomorrow
Dopodomani

Dope Oh Doe Ma Knee

Midnight
Mezzanotte

Met Sun No Tay

Today
Oggi

Oh Gee

Morning
Mattino

Ma Tee No

Month
Mese

May Say

Minute
Minuto

Me New Toe

Century
Secolo

Say Coal Oh

Second
Secondo

Say Cone Doe

Evening
Sera

Said a

Fall
Autunno

A Tune Oh

Computer
Computer

Comb Pewter

Homework
Compiti

Comb Pea Tee

Grade
Voto

Vote Oh

Exercise
Esercizio

Ace Said Cheesey Oh

Idea *Idea*	**Eat Day**
Symbol *Simbolo*	**Seem Bow Low**
Subject *Soggetto*	**Sew Jet Toe**
Experiment *Esperimento*	**Ace Petty Main Toe**

Chapter *Capitolo*	**Cop Pea Toe Low**
Circle *Cerchio*	**Chair Key Oh**
Plus *Più*	**Pea You**
Minus *Meno*	**May No**

HEALTH AND MEDICINE

Pill
Pillola

Pea Lola

Sponge
Spugna

Spoon Ya

Toothbrush
Spazzolino

Spot Sew Lee No

Shampoo
Shampoo

Shampoo

Pulse
Battito

But Tee Toe

Sample
Campione

Come Pea Oh Neigh

Blood
Sangue

Sung Way

Stethoscope
Stetoscopio

Stay Toe Scope Pea Oh

Bush *Cespuglio*	**Chase Pool Yo**
Bouquet *Bouquet*	**Bouquet**
Tulip *Tulipano*	**2 Lee Pa No**
Stem *Gambo*	**Gum Bow**

Poplar
Pioppo

Pea Oh Poe

Lotus
Loto

Low Toe

Pine
Pino

Pea No

Warm *Caldo*	**Call Doe**
Sunny *Sole*	**Sew Lay**
Windy *Vento*	**Vein Toe**
Cloudy *Nuvoloso*	**New Vole Oh Sew**

Hair
Capelli

Cop Pelly

Eyes
Occhi

Oh Key

Stomach
Stomaco

Stow Mock Oh

Knee
Ginocchio

Jean Know Key Oh

Foot
Piede

Pea Aid Day

Head
Testa

Taste a

Neck
Collo

Coal Oh

Skin
Pelle

Pay Lay

Breast
Petto

Pay Toe

Elbow
Gomito

Go Me Toe

Finger
Dito

Dee Toe

Chin
Mento

Main Toe

ENGLITALIANO

All these words are identical in spelling and meaning in English and Italian. Although you may experience small slanguage pronunciation differences, you will still be understood.

- Banana
- Blue
- Bouquet
- Café
- Cappuccino
- Casino
- Cool
- Duo
- Fiasco
- Gelato

- Ghetto
- Gondola
- Gusto
- Hotel
- Jet
- Macaroni
- OK
- Opera
- Pasta
- Piano

- Pizza
- Potpourri
- Prima donna
- Regatta
- Salsa
- Sexy
- Shampoo
- Sofa
- Soprano
- Spaghetti

- Stress
- Studio
- Taxi
- Tempo
- Tuba
- Viola
- Weekend
- Zoo
- Zucchini